Winning Gold

Success Secrets of a World Champion

Lee Kemp

Upaya House Publishing

Cover Design & Layout by Erik Quisling

Cover Photo Credit: Lenspeak (Kyle Flubacker Photography)

Art Direction for Cover Photo Image: Scott Haze
(Photo is from his upcoming film about the life of Lee Kemp.)

Copyright © 2017 by Upaya House Publishing
All Rights Reserved
Library of Congress Cataloging-in-publication Data

Except for appropriate use in critical reviews or works of scholarship, the reproduction or use of this work in any form or by an electronic, mechanical, or other means now known or hereafter invented, including photocopying and recording, and in any information storage and retrieval system is forbidden without the written permission of the publisher.

07 06 05 04 03   5 4 3 2 1   First Edition

Kemp, Lee
    Winning Gold: Success Secrets of a World Champion

Edited by Erik Quisling
    p. cm.

ISBN-10: 1-936965-28-3
ISBN-13: 978-1-936965-28-1

Library of Congress

1. Business 2. Wrestling 3. New Age 4. Self-Help 5. Kemp, Lee

Upaya House Publishing
17465 Calle Mayor / P.O. Box 8716
Rancho Santa Fe, CA 95361

Printed in USA

DEDICATION

I want to dedicate this book to my parents, Leroy and Jesse Kemp. They were daily examples to me, on our farm in Chardon Ohio, of the true essence of the success that determination, dedication and good old-fashioned hard work could bring.

I also want to dedicate this book to all of the coaches and mentors who have guided me in my life. They gave me the inspiration that ultimately led to all of the success that I've had in life both as an athlete and as a human being.

Winning Gold

"Practice like you've never won.
Play like you've never lost."

- Michael Jordan

"Our souls are not hungry for fame, comfort, wealth, or power. Those rewards create almost as many problems as they solve. Our souls are hungry for meaning, for the sense that we have figured out how to live so that our lives matter. So the world will be at least a little bit different for our having passed through it."

- Harold Kushner

Welcome to Winning Gold!

From my earliest recollection I wanted to be great at something. I think it maybe was a subliminal response for needing to feel wanted after being given up at birth and spending the first five years of my life in two foster homes, before being adopted.

I do not remember much about that part of my life other than feeling alone and insignificant. From my adoption records I learned the two foster homes I was in had other children temporarily living there like me, so bonding with anyone was really hard, so I never felt that I belonged anywhere.

As I reflect back I have learned that the struggles and trials I experienced early in my life were actually shaping me for the man I was to become, and without them I certainly would not have had the intense desire to be successful and to feel important and feel like I belonged somewhere.

I believe it was an internal struggle for recognition; to be great at something. This book reflects my thoughts and the things that inspired me along my journey towards success.

I wanted to write down what made me aspire for success out of the hardships and trials we all face every day.

This is a motivational book that will hopefully inspire you to reach higher heights and achieve more than you thought you ever could.

My success story started at age 14, when I was in 9th grade, just nine years out of the foster homes. That was when I went out for and made the freshman wrestling team. The next year I made the varsity squad, and finished the year as an Average wrestler (with a 11 wins, 8 losses, and 3 ties record.)

What happened next was nothing short of remarkable. I completed the next two years as an undefeated two-time Ohio State Wrestling Champion.

This transformation led me on a path to learn the psychological components of not only how to become successful, but how to stay successful.

Consistency was the key to my success and by age 21 I had become the youngest ever American World Champion - a distinction I held for 38 years! I was also America's first 3-Time World Champion.

In only 6 years I went from an Average high school wrestler to World Champion!

The thought process I learned and developed in wrestling is the same for achieving excellence in any vocation or discipline.

I frequently speak to a variety of groups, in both athletic and non-athletic settings, sharing the psychological techniques and strategies I've perfected over the past four decades.

In **Winning Gold,** I have gathered together 75 of my most powerful techniques and strategies and share them with you in the form of my personal Messages.

It is my hope that you can turn to any page of this book and find a message that inspires you!

Message #1

Don't Set Limits on Your Ability or Goals

What are Your Goals?
How Big Are They?

I have a wrestling school and I consistently ask my wrestlers what they want to accomplish.

What I find is that some of them limit their goals to what they think they can achieve, or what they are reasonably sure they can accomplish.

The problem with this is there could be so much more they could accomplish if they only believed in themselves more, and set higher goals.

Never set your limits. When you set your limits, you also set the point where YOU WILL QUIT.

Promise yourself that you will start giving your best effort without setting limits. If you want a breakthrough, stop setting limits!

Get ready to get inspired!!!

Message #2

Whatever You're Going to Do… Do It Now

Don't Wait to Get Started on you Goals... Do It Now... Get Started Now!

Planning is great, but don't plan your success to the point that all you are doing is planning. To put it another way: Don't buy green bananas!

(I hope you get the point.)

Expect results right away. By doing this you will work a little harder. I remember when I first started to lift weights in 8th grade. I could hardly wait until I saw a hint of some muscles starting to develop. I was always pushing for results.

Ability, talent, and opportunity will not produce results all by themselves. You must DO something. There are a lot of people that possess all of these attributes, and more, but they never accomplished much. This is because they never got started on something.

Get started NOW!

Message #3

Every Day You Must Get Up Running

Every day in the Serengeti, a Puma must run faster than the slowest Gazelle to eat, or else he will starve and die…

Every day in the Serengeti, a Gazelle must run faster than the fastest Puma to avoid being eaten, or else he will die…

It doesn't matter who you are in the Serengeti, a Puma or a Gazelle, you better get up running…

-- Ancient African Proverb

Message #4
Dream the Impossible and Believe

They Said it Couldn't be Done...

Roger Bannister had intended to retire after the 1952 Olympics. However, having only come in 4th in the 1500m final he decided to hang on for another two years to make an attempt at the holy grail of middle distance running - the four-minute mile.

Knowing that two other milers had the same intent - John Landy of Australia and Wes Santee of the USA - Bannister ran very early in the season at the Iffley Road track in Oxford.

On May 6, 1954, paced by some old friends, he crossed the finish line in 3 minutes 59.4 seconds, just under the magical time, taking 2 seconds off of Gunder Hägg's nine year old mile World Record.

Amazingly, after all the hype the record only stood for 46 days! John Landy ran 3.57.9 in Finland. Bannister then went on that season to defeat Landy in the "Mile of the Century" in the Empire Games, before winning the European 1500m title. He then retired from the sport at the ripe old age of 25.

It took just 11 years for the first high schooler to break the magical barrier when American, Jim Ryun, clocked the time of 3:55:3 in 1965. To date there has been 10 high school boys that have broken the 4-minute mile.

Nearly sixty years on and it is still one of the most iconic moments in sports history!

Don't believe what others say can or cannot be done!

Message #5

Dream Big!

In 1972, Dan Gable became an Olympic Champion and an instant legend.

In 1976, at the age of 18, I wrestled Dan Gable and won!

I was a sophomore in college with only 6 years of wrestling experience.

There is simply no way I could have entered that match without Dreaming BIG!!!

Message #6

Why People Win

Can you handle the Pressure?

Winning is a function of inner confidence. Successfully dealing with the pressure is a function of the following three things:

1. Training harder than your competition and having superior technique. Really it's about "How prepared are you?" That's the Big 1st question that you must answer before any competition. How you answer this will dictate the rest of the story…

2. Having a disciplined lifestyle resulting in proper eating, nutrition and rest. This is key. It's been said that you can't out train a bad lifestyle. I always felt I had an edge over a competitor that I knew had a bad lifestyle.

3. Having a spiritual focus through prayer and asking God to allow you to perform up to your abilities. That's all you can really do anyway is perform up to your capabilities.

A lot of athletes have not learned how to overcome the anxiety and pressure of a big match and as a result under perform. Pressure and anxiety equate to doubt and uncertainty and that will suck away confidence quicker that anything else.

The more you notice the pressure and anxiety the more you will doubt your abilities and the desired outcome.

Ultimately, it is not about whether you'll win or lose… It's really about whether or not you will PERFORM.

Message #7

How Can I be Sure to Perform?

The best way to be sure of future performance is to do the following:

1. Prepare yourself for your goal by repeatedly challenging and testing yourself in situations similar to the one you want your best performance in.

    This is your "Preparation/Training Time".

    Your "Preparation/Training Time" must have repeated and relentless efforts towards carefully selected goals that continually move upward to "the next level" once lower levels are attained. This keeps you in a state of growth and improvement during your "Preparation/Training Time".

2. Make sure you have enough "Preparation/Training Time" to experience noticeable growth and improvement of your performance during your repeated efforts.

    This is essential for building a solid foundation for your confidence. To put it another way, set goals for yourself that at first seem unattainable during your "Preparation

Time", and put pressure on yourself to not only attain the goals, but to exceed them.

Even though they may seem unattainable allow yourself to feel the emotions and pressure of how your effort stacks up to the goal. This is an important part of the process.

You must allow yourself to feel the emotions and pressure connected with the satisfaction (or disappointment) of your efforts during this "Preparation/Training time".

You want to condition yourself to hunger for the feeling of satisfaction when you've attained one of your "Preparation/Training Time" goals.

3. Continually push and improve each effort toward your goals during the "Preparation /Training Time." Always inch closer towards the ultimate goal you've set for yourself.

Remember, you are trying to do a "dress rehearsal" of your "big event" trying to make it as real as possible. Ultimately, you will evaluate how your repeated effort stacks up to you actually believing your ultimate goal is attainable. The key here is to continually "move the bar higher" improving upon your past practice performances.

4. Draw upon your successes from your "Preparation/Training Time" to establish your history of past successes. This knowledge will provide the foundation for you to actually believe that you can achieve your ultimate goals.

Message #8

Don't Apologize for Trying to Win

Winning is not as Important as a Winning Effort.

"I love to sweat, work and practice…and win.
But to sweat, work and practice…and lose.
I can't see that at all!"

– Lee Kemp

Message #9

Don't Sweat The Small Stuff...

Focus On What's Important NOW.

We are really not that important in the big picture of the universe.

When I visualize of the size of the earth compared to the vastness of the universe it's almost incomprehensible.

Our mortal minds simply can't comprehend the vastness and complexity of the universe combined with the length of time its all been in existence.

Our mere human life span of an average of 80 years makes us a really insignificant blip in this incomprehensible continuum.

With all of this complexity created by God, the Bible says we are all made in God's image.

Wow!!! This is incredibly humbling. Don't spend another moment sweating the small stuff in Life…

FOCUS on What's Important NOW!

Message #10

"Burn the Ships"

Commitment is the foundation of all success.

The phrase "Burn The Ships" comes from folklore and I love the story and the example it brings.

The phrase is actually attributed to Spanish Conquistador Hernando Cortez. In 1519, Cortez and his men landed in Mexico on the shores of the Yucatan with only one objective... seize the great Aztec treasures known to be hoarded there.

Cortez's commitment to this mission and his quest for riches is legendary. An excellent motivator, he convinced more than 500 soldiers and 100 sailors to set sail from Spain to Mexico, commanding 11 ships, to take the world's richest treasure.

The historic question is "how a small band of 500 Spanish soldiers arrived in a strange country and swiftly brought about the overthrow of a large and powerful empire that was in power for more than six centuries?"

For Cortez, the answer was easy. It was all or nothing! A Complete and Total Commitment. Here's how Cortez got the "buy in" from the rest of his men. He took away the option of failure. It was conquer and be heroes and enjoy the spoils of victory...or DIE!

When Cortez and his men arrived on the shores of the Yucatan he rallied the men for one final pep talk before leading them into battle. It was here that he uttered the three words that would change the course of history.

"Burn the Ships!"

At first he met with resistance from his men.

"Burn the ships!" he repeated. "If we are going home, we are going home in their ships!"

With that, Cortez and his men burned their own ships, and by burning their own ships, the commitment level of the men was raised to a whole new level. A level much higher than any of the men, including Cortez, could have ever imagined.

Amazingly, the men conquered the Aztecs and had succeeded in something where others had been unsuccessful for six centuries. With the victory Cortez and his men took the treasure.

Why did they win? They had no escape. No fall back position. They had no choice! It was "succeed or die." Their ships were burned. They had no way to get back. Their backs were to the wall.

To really succeed you must have an attitude much like that of Cortez and his men. Cortez and his men did not have a "crutch" or "fall back position." They frankly didn't have any options. It was simply "succeed or DIE." Pretty strong position, isn't it? How would you like to be engaged in fighting someone with that level of motivation and commitment?

This is the level of motivation and commitment you must have - the "BURN YOUR SHIPS" level of motivation and commitment. Take away your crutches and excuses and burn the ships that are keeping you from achieving your goals. Identity the ships in your life that are keeping you from accomplishing dreams. I have two sayings that I live by: One is "Dream Big." The other is "Burn your Ships."

Whatever prevents you from achieving your goals and dreams are ships that must be burned. Not dismantled, or run ashore…but burned and destroyed! If we know that our ships are still out there, when things get tough we instinctively head for our ships so we can escape. It's just human nature to take the path of least resistance. This level of thinking and commitment sees sacrifice as a positive thing, not something weird or impossible, but something to be cherished and fought for.

Cortez didn't allow himself or his men to have the option of going back to Spain. By removing this option, Cortez and his men were forced to focus on how they could make the mission successful. And so it is with you. How can you make the missions in your life successful?

This is really a story about commitment. Commitment is the foundation of success. Not a single accomplishment is ever achieved without it. By focusing on commitment, we seal our future.

Message #11

The Battle Inside of All of Us

TWO WOLVES

One evening an old Cherokee told his grandson about a battle that goes on inside people.

He said, "My son, the battle is between two wolves inside us all. One is Evil. It is anger, envy, jealousy, sorrow, regret, greed, arrogance, self-pity, guilt, resentment, inferiority, lies, false pride, superiority, and ego. The other is Good. It is joy, peace, love, hope, serenity, humility, kindness, benevolence, empathy, generosity, truth, compassion and faith."

The grandson thought about it for a minute and then asked his grandfather, "Which wolf wins?"

The old Cherokee simply replied, "The one you feed."

       - Ancient Native American Metaphor

Message #12

Burning Your Ships… Ali Style

This is How Muhammad Ali Burned His Ships.

You don't have to be a Muhammad Ali fan to appreciate his desire to win and the supreme confidence he displayed when preparing for his boxing matches in the ring.

His signature tag line of "I'm the Greatest" is legendary. Even the Ali detractors grew to respect his great courage and desire to be the best.

Quite simply, it all boiled down to winning.

Muhammad Ali would make outrageous statements about his opponents and about what he would do if he lost. He left himself no way out. He had only one thing to think about, and that was how he was going to WIN! Losing was not an option for him. He took that option away by his antics.

Think of the pressure you would feel if you backed yourself into a corner like he did, saying all that crazy stuff he used to say. Think of how hard and intensely you would train. Think of the depth and scope of your mental preparation necessary to avoid the humiliation of having to eat your words if you lost.

Any way you look at it, this is "Burning Your Ships"…you win or else you'll be humiliated.

In 1964, Ali had his biggest fight at the time – a shot at the heavyweight world title. It was against Sonny

Liston, the most feared heavyweight in the world and if he lost this fight his career would have suffered a great setback. To say the least, it possibly could have ended his career. The media would never have taken him seriously after that, and more importantly, how could he have taken himself seriously after that.

We all know what happened. Ali went on to beat Sonny Liston to become the youngest Heavyweight Boxing Champion in History.

This is not just positive thinking but POSITIVE BELIEVING.

Message #13

Dreaming Big! (Shackleton Style)

Sir Ernest Shackleton and the Endurance.

In December of 1914, Sir Ernest Shackleton set sail on "The Endurance" with his 27-man crew to accomplish something that had never been done before. He wanted to be the first man to completely cross the Antarctic continent on foot.

This was an extremely dangerous mission and to select many of the 27-man crew, it is said, they had responded to the following recruitment notice:

"Men wanted for hazardous journey. Small wages. Bitter cold. Long months of complete darkness. Constant danger. Safe return doubtful. Honor and recognition in case of success." - Ernest Shackleton.

Icy conditions were unusually harsh at the start of the journey, and the wooden ship - which Shackleton had renamed Endurance after his family motto, Fortitudine Vincimus "by endurance we conquer," – had become trapped in the pack ice of the Weddell Sea.

For 10 months, the Endurance drifted, locked within the ice, until the pressure crushed the ship. With meager food, clothing and shelter, Shackleton and his men were stranded on the ice floes, where they camped for five months.

When they had drifted to the northern edge of the

ice pack, encountering open leads of water, the men sailed the three small lifeboats they'd salvaged to a bleak crag called Elephant Island.

They were on land for the first time in 497 days but it was uninhabited and, due to its distance from shipping lanes, provided no hope for rescue.

Recognizing the severity of the physical and mental strains on his men, Shackleton and five others immediately set out to take the crew's rescue into their own hands. In a 22-foot lifeboat named the James Caird, they accomplished the impossible, surviving a 17-day, 800-mile journey through the world's worst seas to South Georgia Island, where a whaling station was located.

Unfortunately, the six men landed on the wrong side of the island and their only hope to get to the whaling station was to cross 26 miles of mountains and glaciers that were long considered impassable.

Against these odds, Shackleton and two others made the trek, and on the afternoon of May 20, 1916, they miraculously arrived at South Georgia's Stromness whaling station.

Starved, frostbitten and wearing rags, they had marched non-stop for 36 hours. When they walked through the doors of the station they were unrecognizable. The station manager there asked, "Who the hell are you?"

"My name is Shackleton," was the modest reply,

and he immediately began making plans plans to rescue the Elephant Island group.

The Norwegians volunteered a ship but 60 miles from Elephant Island, the ice prevented the unprotected vessel from continuing.

As the months passed, Shackleton made increasingly frantic rescue attempts, each time thwarted by ice or weather.

At last, on August 30, they succeeded in bringing through a tug boat loaned to them by the Chilean government named the Yelcho. It would be their fourth attempt.

Four months had passed since the Caird's departure, and Shackleton feared the worst.

On Elephant Island, the Yelcho was spotted. As the castaways ran onto the beach, Shackleton, straining through binoculars, counted anxiously. "They are all there!" Worsley reported him crying.

On August 1916, 21 months after the initial departure of the Endurance, Shackleton returned to rescue the men on Elephant Island. Although they'd withstood the most incredible hardship and deprivation, not one member of the 28-man crew was lost.

Shackleton was quoted as saying "If anything had happened to those fellows while waiting for me, I would have felt like a murderer."

Message #14

Attitude

A Powerful Message on Attitude from Pastor Chuck Swindoll:

"We are all in charge of our attitudes."

THE LONGER I LIVE, THE MORE I REALIZE THE IMPACT OF ATTITUDE ON LIFE.

ATTITUDE, TO ME, IS MORE IMPORTANT THAN FACTS.

IT IS MORE IMPORTANT THAN THE PAST, THAN EDUCATION, THAN MONEY, THAN CIRCUMSTANCES, THAN FAILURES, THAN SUCCESSES, THAN WHAT OTHER PEOPLE THINK, OR SAY, OR DO.

IT IS MORE IMPORTANT THAN APPEARANCE, GIFTEDNESS, OR SKILL.

IT WILL MAKE OR BREAK A COMPANY…A CHURCH…A HOME.

THE REMARKABLE THING IS WE HAVE A CHOICE EVERY DAY REGARDING THE ATTITUDE WE WILL EMBRACE FOR THAT DAY.

WE CANNOT CHANGE OUR PAST…WE CANNOT CHANGE THE FACT THAT PEOPLE WILL ACT IN A CERTAIN WAY.

WE CANNOT CHANGE THE INEVITABLE.

THE ONLY THING WE CAN DO IS PLAY ON THE ONE THING WE HAVE, AND THAT IS OUR ATTITUDE.

I AM CONVINCED THAT LIFE IS 10% WHAT HAPPENS TO ME AND 90% HOW I REACT TO IT.

AND SO IT IS WITH YOU…WE ARE IN CHARGE OF OUR ATTITUDES.

–Chuck Swindoll

Message #15

Dreaming Big! (Jamill Kelly Style)

**Never quit and never give up!
You never know when your breakthrough is coming!**

As a wrestler, Jamill Kelly Never won a state title and he never even placed in the NCAA's.

But deep down inside, Jamill Kelly always believed that someday he would WIN BIG…and he DID!

Jamill made the 2003 World Team and made the 2004 Olympic team by beating opponents that won a combined total of 5 NCAA Titles.

Jamill went on to earn a silver medal in the 2004 Olympic Games by beating several previous World and Olympic Medalists!

Message #16

Opposition and Hardships

Character determines What You Will Choose, Where You Will Go, What You Will Do, When You Will Quit, What You Will Say, When You Will Compromise, How You Will Live and ultimately What You Will Achieve.

"The ultimate measure of a man is not where he stands in moments of comfort and convenience, but where he stands at times of challenge and controversy". – Martin Luther King, Jr.

This quote by Martin Luther King, Jr., symbolizes what the true measure of a person is.

IT IS WHERE THEY STAND WHEN THINGS GET HARD; WHEN THINGS AREN'T SAFE; WHEN THINGS AREN'T CONVENIENT; WHEN THINGS ARE DIFFICULT.

And so it is with anything you want to do or accomplish in life. If you want it…be prepared to fight for it. They don't sell GOLD MEDALS or PURPLE HEARTS at the department store. You won't find them at garage sales either. You'll find them buried deep within the souls of men and women passionate about accomplishing their mission.

Once you set out on your mission, there's no turning back. You can't look back…only forward. Even when you stumble, you must stumble forward.

"Great accomplishments are only attained by overcoming great obstacles. THE GREATER THE OBSTACLE… THE GREATER THE ACCOMPLISHMENT." - Anonymous

This quote hung in our wrestling room and I looked at it every day. I made sure I challenged and tested myself every day by somehow making every practice harder than the day before (these were the obstacles.) By conquering them I felt my confidence growing stronger until I believed there was no obstacle I couldn't overcome.

"You can measure a man by the opposition it takes to discourage him". – Robert C. Savage

Message #17

Are You On the Move?

All of us are either moving towards our goals and dreams… or moving farther away from them. We are never in a holding pattern. Can you handle the pressure?

Think about this. Pick one goal that's important to you.

Are you closer to achieving this goal or are you farther away from achieving this goal, this year vs. last year (this month vs. last month; this week vs. last week; today vs. yesterday.)

Be honest with yourself. Talk to yourself. Look at yourself in the mirror as you talk to yourself. What do you see? Do you see a person that's fighting to stay in the "game" or a person who is standing on the sideline.

If you're closer to achieving this goal, ask yourself why? On a separate piece of paper, list at least 5 things you did to get you closer to your goal.

If you're farther away from achieving this goal, again ask yourself why? List at least 5 things you failed to do that slowed your progress towards your goal.

LOOK AT YOUR LISTS. WHAT DO YOU SEE? PICK OTHER GOALS AND DO THE LISTS. DO YOU SEE ANY PATTERNS DEVELOPING…?

This is simple and hard at the same time. Seems simple to just do more of the things that lead to success and less of the things that lead to failure.

The question becomes… How do we get motivated to do the things that lead to success?

The answer is to live in the present and in the NOW!

Everyone that's got to where they are had to start from where they were. Most people at first see the goal and get discouraged because they don't see results quickly enough. Or they become preoccupied with the small setbacks and failures that we all have when we set out to do something.

WHAT CAN YOU DO RIGHT NOW TO MOVE YOU CLOSER TO ONE OF YOUR GOALS?

WHAT CAN YOU ELIMINATE RIGHT NOW THAT HAS BEEN GETTING IN THE WAY OF YOU ACHIEVING ONE OF YOUR GOALS?

**FIND OUT WHAT'S IMPORTANT NOW…
AND DO IT!**

Message #18

Over and Above Your Expectations

What Would You Accomplish If you knew you could not fail?

What if you had the revelation that anything you tried would be successful? WHAT THEN WOULD YOU SET OUT TO DO?

Would you set out to discover the cure for the deadliest cancers known to the world?

Would you strive to break a record that was said could never be broken?

Would you go to medical school?
Would you try out for the varsity team?
Would you try out for the Olympic Team?
Would you make an attempt to repair a broken relationship?
Would you attempt to create something that has never existed before?
Would you set out to climb Mt. Everest?

WHAT ARE YOU WAITING FOR?

EVERY GREAT ACCOMPLISHMENT STARTED OUT WITH SMALL FAILURES ALONG HE WAY.

IT'S THE CONVICTION TO THE LONG-TERM GOAL THAT ALLOWS YOU TO OVERLOOK THE SMALL FAILURES.

ACT IS IF YOU COULD ACCOMPLISH ANYTHING YOU SET OUT TO DO!

Message #19

What is Commitment?

Remember the story about the chicken and the pig, and how they contribute to our Breakfast?

Providing eggs is a small sacrifice for the chicken but providing bacon is a total commitment for the Pig.

Joking aside. There is great power in making a commitment.

People often think because they are making some sacrifices (large or small) towards a goal that they are committed to the goal; when in fact they are not really committed at all.

Sacrifices and Commitments are different...very different!

Sacrifices may get you in the game but commitments get the job done!

Making sacrifices are a lot like making promises: when things get tough, promises are often broken and sacrifices are often stopped.

What separates sacrifices and promises from commitments is that commitments are never broken or stopped.

Sounds tough when you hear it like that.

Unless a commitment is made, there are only promises and hopes and maybe a little sacrifice.... but no plan of definite action and uncompromising will to succeed.

The one common denominator for all personal achievement is a person's ability to make a commitment (to themselves) to do what ever it takes to achieve the Goal.

It's the "Burn Your Ships" attitude.

Remember, commitments are NEVER BROKEN.

Chickens and pigs look at life differently… which are you?

Message #20

Life Is A Gift – Live it, Embrace It, and Remember The One Who Gives Life

Live Life to the Fullest. Don't Settle for Less. Life is Too Precious to Settle for Less.

"Life Is a Gift"

Today before you say an unkind word…Think of someone who can't speak.

Before you complain about the taste of your food…Think of someone who has nothing to eat.

Before you complain about your husband or wife…Think of someone who's crying out to GOD for a companion.

Today before you complain about life …Think of someone who went too early to heaven.

Before you complain about your children…Think of someone who desires children but they're barren.

Before you argue about your dirty house someone didn't clean or sweep…Think of the people who are living in the streets.

Before whining about the distance you drive…Think of someone who walks the same distance with their feet.

And when you are tired and complain about your job…Think of the unemployed, the disabled, and those who wish they had your job.

But before you think of pointing the finger or condemning another...Remember that not one of us are without sin and we all answer to one MAKER.

And when depressing thoughts seem to get you down -Put a smile on your face and thank GOD you're alive and still around.

Life is a gift, Live it, Enjoy it, Celebrate it, And Fulfill it.

We Serve an AWESOME GOD !!!!!!

Message #21

Dreaming Big! (Wilma Rudolph Style)

This is an amazing story about one of America's greatest athletes and her mother!

On June 23, 1940, Wilma Rudolph was born in Clarksville, Tennessee.

Having been born prematurely and weighing only 4.5 pounds, little Wilma was susceptible to illness and her mother spent several years nursing her through measles, mumps, and scarlet fever. One day her family noticed that Wilma's left foot was becoming weak. Her mother took her to the doctor who informed them that Wilma had polio and would never walk.

Wilma's mother refused to accept the diagnosis. She had something special in her heart – she had the power of belief and she told her young daughter that one day she would walk. Twice a week for the next two years, she took her daughter for treatment to a hospital that was more than 50 miles away.

The doctors at the hospital taught Mrs. Rudolph how to perform the physical therapy exercises Wilma needed and every night she would massage her daughter's legs late into the evening.

Wilma progressed slowly but steadily. By the time she was seven she could walk with the aid of metal leg braces.

At school, Wilma sat and watched the other children

running and told herself that one day she too would enjoy the freedom of being able to run.

In 1952, 12-year old Wilma finally threw away her metal leg braces and was able to walk without assistance for the first time. It was then that she made the decision to be an athlete.

She started to play basketball and also did some running in the offseason to keep fit. As time progressed, Wilma became a basketball star, setting state records and leading her team to a state championship.

During one basketball match, Wilma was spotted by the Tennessee State track and field coach, Edward Temple. He was amazed by Wilma's athletic ability. With coach Temple's help, Wilma turned her focus from basketball to running and she never looked back.

By the time she was 16, Wilma had earned a spot on the US Olympic track and field team and won a bronze medal in the 4×100m relay at the 1956 Melbourne Olympics.

Four years later, Wilma Rudolph won three Olympic Gold medals at the 1960 Rome Olympics in the 100m, 200m and 4×100m relay. The little girl who was once crippled was now "The fastest woman in history."

"I ran and ran and ran every day, and I acquired this

sense of determination, this sense of spirit that I would never, never give up, no matter what else happened." – Wilma Rudolph

When you DREAM BIG…anything is possible!

Message #22

Love the Process

Winning Does Not Lead to Passion; Passion Leads to Winning.

You must absolutely love the process in order for this success principle to work.

You're wondering "WHAT IS THE PROCESS?"

Well, the process is EVERYTHING that comes before the success. This includes the PRACTICE time; the REHEARSAL time; the DRILLING time; the LEARNING time; the GETTING THE DETAILS RIGHT time; the REBOUNDING AFTER A SET BACK time; the OVERCOMING A BAD CALL time; the REHABILITATION AFTER AN INJURY time; the THINKING ABOUT QUITTING time.

All in all, you must love the PROCESS in order to reach the highest goal possible.

It is the LOVE of the PROCESS that separates the mere team members (whatever the team - sports, business, whatever) from the State, National and World Champions! Granted the champions are team members too, but before the champions became champions they first LOVED the process.

Think about this. I've read that when Michael Jordan played, his love for the game of basketball was so great that he would have played for nothing (in fact he had a "love of the game clause" in his contract that allowed him to play basketball whenever and where ever he wanted.) Larry Bird has said the same thing. Other great achievers in various disciplines have said the same thing..."they would have worked and toiled at their craft regardless of any reward."

Quite simply, THEY LOVED THE PROCESS, and by loving the process they were able to achieve great success.

In the case of Michael and Larry, it was their PASSION for the game of basketball that paved the way for them to become great basketball players.

This is going to sound crazy, but these two great basketball players in my opinion, Michael Jordan and Larry Bird, actually loved the game more than they loved WINNING. Think about Michael's career with the Chicago Bulls - how he hung in there all those losing years with the Bulls despite the fact that he himself was playing really great basketball. It was his great love of the game that came before the great periods of winning.

A lot of good athletes in high school sometimes fail to excel when they get to college, or even quit their sport after they get to college. I believe these athletes realized they were going to have to "climb the mountain" again and do all the work necessary to get back on top (just like they did in High School), and when they realized this they didn't want to do it again.

IT IS A LOVE OF THE PROCESS THAT IS THE FOUNDATION FOR SUCCESS.

Message #23

Breaking Through Fear

In war it has been said that there are only two types of soldiers – those with courage and those without courage. Those with courage are sometimes called heroes and those without are sometimes called cowards.

No one likes to talk about FEAR in sports (and War) because it somehow makes us seem weak and wimpy. The fact is everyone feels fear. And certainly no one wants to be called a coward. The connection here is Contact and Combat sports are much like war. The more violent the situation – the more it's like war.

Wrestling and even more so, MMA fighting, are like war.

The mind senses the stress of the situation and involuntarily signals the fear emotion. Since the fear emotion is involuntary and out of our control, the reality is, EVERYONE FEELS FEAR.

In war the HEROES respond, act and perform appropriately, according to their preparation and training, and they do all this at the right time… RIGHT ACTION, RIGHT TIME.

Quite simply, those who lack courage feel the same fear but either don't act or don't act appropriately, or if they do act – they act at the wrong time, and ultimately miss the opportunity.

WRONG ACTION, WRONG TIME.

Frankly, we've all felt like cowards at one time or another haven't we? I know I have. We simply froze and didn't act (or perform like we've trained.) We knew we were hesitating and shutting down, but felt we could do nothing about it.

Since FEAR is felt by all, then HOW does the Hero perform with courage while others become paralyzed and fail?

HAVING COURAGE IS NOT THE ABSENCE OF FEAR, BUT THE ABILITY TO FEEL THE FEAR AND ACT AND PERFORM ANYWAY!

IT'S A CHOICE. HEROES DON'T PLAN TO BE HEROES. THEY JUST SIMPLY ACT AND PERFORM IN THE HEAT OF THE MOMENT, IN SPITE OF THE OBSTACLES AND CIRCUMSTANCES.

TELL YOURSELF YOU WILL ACT AND PERFORM NO MATTER WHAT!

Message #24

Start with A Blank Canvas...And Paint Your Future

"Speed of the Ship is the Speed of the Captain."

Over the years I've noticed that this quote is true, not only with my life but also in the lives of others. If you want to find out where a team, business or any organization is going, just simply take the time to meet the people in charge.

The same is true for each of us as individuals. I can tell you where an individual is going by simply spending some time with them and observing their "speed."

I don't want to sound judgmental but a person's actions speak much louder than their words.

I get asked all the time by younger wrestlers "What do I have to do to become a good wrestler?"

I always answer this question the same way by answering with this question, "What are you doing now to become a good wrestler?" The wrestler's answer is almost always the same, "Well I'm not doing anything yet."

Then I ask the "killer" question, "Have you ever been to a camp or clinic and been inspired by hearing an accomplished wrestler or athlete tell their success story?" The answer is usually "yes".

Then I ask, "Why haven't you started doing the things that you heard this accomplished person say they did to have greater success?" The answer is usually "I don't know."

This, to me, is like standing in front of your "success canvas" and putting your paint brush down and leaving all the colors in their containers, and staring at your canvas and wondering why it doesn't change for you.

The inspiration has to come from within *and be sustained.* There can be a catalyst, like a motivational talk, to ignite the inspiration, but is has to be sustained from within.

If you do what you've always done, you'll get what you always got. If you're not happy with where you're at then start with a "blank canvas" and dream and paint…then dream some more and paint…then dream some more and paint…you get the "picture."

Message #25

Having The Right Attitude

The difference between having the right attitude and almost having the right attitude is the difference between lightning and the lightning bug!

Over the years I've noticed that this statement is true. What do I mean by that? Well there is a heck of a big difference between what lightning can do and what a bug can do. Lightning really sounds powerful until the word bug is added to it. Lightning and Lightning Bug sound like they could be similar until you examine what they both can do; then you conclude they are not close at all.

The same is true when we have a Lightning Bug Attitude: A little flash that's only visible when it's dark outside. But when Lightning flashes across the sky it doesn't matter how much daylight is present - it lights up the entire sky and is clearly seen by all. Lightning never goes unnoticed.

When we come up short in a task or fail to achieve a goal we find solace in thinking "well, I was close." We all know being close doesn't count really. We need the lightning and not the lightning bug.

We see the "Light" in our mind's eye that tells us we're giving our best effort. But is the light we see coming from our effort a Lighting Bolt, or just the glow from a Lightning Bug. Not all "Light" is as bright nor is the same.

Attitude is the key driver of success and achievement.

Be a lightning bolt. Light up the place with your effort and attitude. Let your effort soar to heights you never thought possible because the power of your attitude was just like lightning... Limitless and Powerful!

Which do you have in your attitude - Lightning or just a lighting bug?

Message #26

See The Possibilities Before They Become Obvious

Don't be detoured by the doubters and naysayers. Your future is made up of the things you dream about now…DREAM BIG!!!!

Consider these statements by "so called" experts:

"Babe Ruth made a big mistake when he gave up pitching." - Tris Speaker, 1927.

"I'm just glad it'll be Clark Gable who's falling on his face and not Gary Cooper." - Gary Cooper on his decision not to take the leading role in "Gone With The Wind."

"Who the hell wants to hear actors talk?" - H.M. Warner, Warner Brothers, 1927.

"We don't like their sound, and guitar music is on the way out." - Decca Recording Co. rejecting the Beatles, 1962.

"A cookie store is a bad idea. Besides, the market research reports say America likes crispy cookies, not soft and chewy cookies like you make." - Response to Debbi Fields' idea of starting Mrs. Fields' Cookies.

"There is no reason anyone would want a computer in their home." - Ken Olson, president, chairman and founder of Digital Equipment Corp., 1977.

"The concept is interesting and well-formed, but in

order to earn better than a 'C,' the idea must be feasible." - A Yale University management professor in response to Fred Smith's paper proposing reliable overnight delivery service. (Smith went on to found Federal Express Corp) .

This 'telephone' has too many shortcomings to be seriously considered as a means of communication. The device is inherently of no value to us." - Western Union internal memo, 1876.

"You should change your major to Phys. Ed, the Business School is too tough for you" - A professor's response to Lee Kemp when he was seeking help in one of his business classes (Lee Kemp not only earned a Bachelor's Degree in Business but a Masters of Business Degree (MBA) 1977.

"The wireless music box has no imaginable commercial value. Who would pay for a message sent to nobody in particular?" - David Sarnoff's associates in response to his urgings for investment in the radio in the 1920s.

"Heavier-than-air flying machines are impossible." - Lord Kelvin, president, Royal Society, 1895.

"The United States will never beat the Russians in Greco Roman Wrestling" - The general sentiment and consensus of "so called" wrestling experts of our day (The United States did the impossible, and won the team title in the 2008 World Greco Roman

Wrestling Championships, in Baku Azerbaijan, by beating the Russian Team).

"If I had thought about it, I wouldn't have done the experiment. The literature was full of examples that said you can't do this." - Spencer Silver on the work that led to the unique adhesives for 3-M "Post-It" Note pads.

"So we went to Atari and said, 'Hey, we've got this amazing thing, even built with some of your parts, and what do you think about funding us? Or we'll give it to you. We just want to do it. Pay our salary, we'll come work for you.' And they said, 'No.' So then we went to Hewlett-Packard, and they said, 'Hey, we don't need you. You haven't got through college yet.'" - Apple Computer Inc. founder Steve Jobs on attempts to get Atari and H-P interested in his and Steve Wozniak's personal computer.

"You want to have consistent and uniform muscle development across all of your muscles? It can't be done. It's just a fact of life. You just have to accept inconsistent muscle development as an unalterable condition of weight training." - Response to Arthur Jones, who solved the "unsolvable" problem by inventing Nautilus.

"Don't set your goal that high, you'll only be disappointed when you don't reach it" - A coach's response to Lee Kemp's goal of wanting to be the first 4-time NCAA Champion 1974 (a split referee's decision in overtime prevented Lee Kemp from achieving that goal).

"Drill for oil? You mean drill into the ground to try and find oil? You're crazy." - Drillers who Edwin L. Drake tried to enlist to his project to drill for oil in 1859.

"Stocks have reached what looks like a permanently high plateau." - Irving Fisher, Professor of Economics, Yale University, 1929 (before the great stock market of 1930).

"Airplanes are interesting toys but of no military value." - Marechal Ferdinand Foch, Professor of Strategy, Ecole Superieure de Guerre.

"64K ought to be enough for anybody." - Bill Gates, 1981.

"I think there is a world market for maybe five computers." - Thomas Watson, chairman of IBM, 1943.

"But what is it good for?" - Engineer at the Advanced Computing Systems Division of IBM, 1968, commenting on the microchip.

"I have traveled the length and breadth of this country and talked with the best people, and I can assure you that data processing is a fad that won't last out the year." - The editor in charge of business books for Prentice Hall, 1957.

I think you get the picture...

Message #27

Do Your Actions Mirror Your Words?

Stop and think about several important things you SAID you were going to do. DID YOU DO THEM? What attempts did you make to do them? How PASSIONATE were you in trying to do them?

You get my point. Say Less and DO MORE. Keep track of what you say and reconcile it with what you actually DO.

I'm not talking about things like "I'm going to win this tournament" or "I'm going to land this big business deal" or "I'm going to discover the cure for cancer."

Truth is, we can't predict the future so we really don't know what's going to happen.

What I am talking about are things like:

"I'm going to bust my but today at practice and give it everything I've got."

"I'm going to study everyday for eight hours so that I can be as prepared as possible to pass the exam."

"I will help someone in need today."

"I will not get angry today no matter what happens."

"I will be positive today no matter what happens"

"I will not give up today on anything even if it gets unbelievably hard."

You get the point. These kinds of affirmations are totally in our control and are predictable.

The question becomes…do we actually do what's in our control OR do we make excuses and turn our talk into just that…TALK.

Do we walk the talk?

SAY LESS AND DO MORE…AND DO WHAT YOU SAY YOU ARE GOING TO DO.

Message #28

Resist the Feelings of Fear and Doubt and Perform Anyway

Consistent performance requires resisting the feelings of fear, uncertainty and doubt in the midst of challenge, controversy and disappointment.

I heard a story that exemplifies this principle:

A well-known circus performer was performing his act with several large Bengal tigers in a locked cage before a live audience when, in the middle of his performance, the lights went out.

For almost 30 seconds the circus performer was locked in with the tigers, in total darkness, with the audience starting to panic. The tigers, with their superb night vision, could see him, but he could not see them. The circus performer survived the ordeal, and when the lights came back on he finished his performance.

After the performance the circus performer admitted he was afraid and felt immense and overwhelming fear. However, he said he knew that even though he couldn't see the big tigers, they didn't know he couldn't see them. The circus performer acted in the cage as if nothing had happened and continued cracking his whip and talking to the tigers as he normally would until the lights came back on.

The circus performer relied on the fact that the tigers never knew he couldn't see them. And so it is with each of us. Resist the urge to panic and feel despair in the midst of a "storm" in your life, and perform exactly as you were trained and exactly as you've prepared ahead of time.

Act in faith that your actions will be successful if you simply just carry them out exactly as planned.

Message #29

It's All In Your Mind

You are what you think about.

Think about the last time you were having a so-called "bad day." Identify the sequences of events, and more importantly, the resulting thoughts you had from the events, that led up to you concluding you were having a "bad day."

What you will find is, when something happens to us that we don't like, we attached a bad thought or feeling to it. And conversely, when something happens to us that we like, we attach a good (or positive) thought or feeling to it.

This process just described puts us at the mercy of events and things that happen to us. If on a given day more bad things are happening to us than good things, we begin to think, feel, and say "I'm having a bad day." And the opposite is also true.

The problem is, what if you have something very important that you want to do or accomplish and you're having a so-called "bad day?" Does your important accomplishment, by default, get automatically included in the "bad day" you're already having?

I'll show you how you can avoid this from happening.

First you must start separating feelings and thoughts from events, and let your thoughts and resulting feelings STAND ON THEIR OWN, independent of any event.

When thoughts and resulting feelings are attached to an event, the event can and will dictate your feelings.

So if you are feeling bad as a result of negative events it will be impossible to perform at your best level at anything you endeavor to accomplish. I have witnessed people going through incredibly difficult events, but they seemed to still have JOY and inner peace. They may not have been happy, but they had an uncompromising joy and exuberance for life that couldn't be quenched.

Happiness is very different than JOY. Happiness IS based on what's happening to you – but JOY isn't. For example, you're not going to be happy if you find out you have cancer but you can have the knowledge that you are still the same person as before you received the bad news. You still possess the same intelligence, talent, charm, and personality, desire and will before and after the bad news.

Allowing an event to affect your JOY and the essence of who you are is a CHOICE. It's YOUR CHOICE. Don't let an event or another person make that choice for you.

I use the cancer example because I've met people that are battling cancer right now, and I'm amazed at how positive these people are about life and about themselves. You see, these people have not let their circumstance or negative events in their life define who they are, or steal their JOY of living, or diminish their desire to accomplish things.

If you string together enough bad thoughts as a result of negative feelings derived from negative things that happen to you, I guarantee that you will end up concluding "you are having a bad day."

Message #30

Stretch your Mind

Once Something is Stretched it never Goes Back to the Way it was Before.

Anything you actually do is first contemplated (or incubated) as a thought in your mind. When you let your mind dwell on a thought long enough something very powerful happens - YOU BEGIN TO GRAVITATE TOWARDS IT.

What do I mean by this? Think about anything you've ever accomplished and you'll agree it first started with a thought that came into your mind that you formed into a goal. The greater the goal the more time you will spend thinking about it. The time spent thinking about the goal will be greater than anything else you think about… you will spend a disproportionate amount of time thinking about it compared to everything else.

There are many ways thoughts come into our minds. We are bombarded with all kinds of images, messages and situations. The moment we fixate on one of them we form a thought about it.

If the thought is something we desire, we immediately rationalize and assess how realistic it is to attain it. This is where most people fail. If they think they can't attain the goal they let the thought go and start thinking about something else.

The reason why successful people realize their goals is that they keep the desired goal in their mind as a thought, and continually keep it there.

Sometimes these people are characterized as one-dimensional or one-track minded.

I CALL THESE PEOPLE CHAMPIONS!

By doing this you are in effect "stretching" your mind.   Once you do this you will never be the same!

Message #31

Your Ultimate Goal Must be Burned in Your Mind

Keep Your Goal Constantly in Focus to Keep You From Being Frustrated by Set Backs and Failures Along the Way... Remember, Keep Your Eyes Fixed on the Prize!

No matter what happens you must not forget why you're in the game: TO WIN! And winning is whatever you have defined it to be.

Remember the old saying, "It's not over till it's over". No matter how many times you fail at something... you only have to succeed at it ONCE! That's it... ONLY ONCE. You only have to do it right once...no matter how many times you've failed at it.

It took George Eastman (of Eastman-Kodak) 18 years to perfect the film process to achieve his ultimate dream and goal of making photography available to the average person.

He set out in 1877 with his dream and didn't achieve it until 1895. He endured over 1,000 flawed and failed experiments perfecting the film process, worked a day job at a bank to pay the bills, read books on chemistry and photography to increase his knowledge, learned French and German so he could read the latest research about the film industry, and spent many nights sleeping in a hammock at his factory after long days designing equipment.

George Eastman never lost sight of his goal...How about YOU!

Message #32

Visualization is a Really Powerful Tool

Don't Just Say it... Don't Just Believe it... VISUALIZE IT AS IF IT'S ACTUALLY HAPPENING!

Your Visualization goes beyond just believing. Believing is GREAT, don't get me wrong. But visualizing something takes it to a higher level and unleashes unbelievable power.

Put the desired goal in your mind and experience every facet of it like your favorite movie, played in slow motion, picking up every detail, every subtlety, every frame.

The secret here is that you can visualize your successful attainment of the goal. It's your movie to direct, so direct it with you coming out on top... winning! Play this movie over, and over, and over, and over... you get the picture.

Scientific research supports that the mind can actually fool the body (including the emotions) into believing something that hasn't actually happened yet. How many times have we woken up from a dream and were amazed at how real it all seemed?

The trick is to guide your visualization into the place you want.

Message #33

Gaining an Edge

How to Get an Edge on the Competition

What are you willing to do to gain the things you want?

Are you willing to be positive when things aren't going your way?

Are you willing to do the things that are hard?

Are you willing to work harder than anyone else?

Are you willing to continually learn about your craft?

Are you willing to accept constructive criticism?

Are you willing to do the things no one else wants to do?

I have one question for every one reading this post right now...

What are you willing to do today and tomorrow that gives you an EDGE over your competition?

I coach a group of wrestlers that work out on Christmas Eve and Christmas Day!

Message #34

Stay Focused on Your Goals

Be Prepared to Be Tested...

What is a TEST?

A test is when you are challenged...when you doubt... when you stumble...when you don't succeed at first... when you feel like quitting... when you fail... when you think you're not good enough... when you get sick... when you get tired... when you are wondering how in the world are you're going to do this.

But a test is also a chance to reaffirm your commitment to your goal.

Welcome any and all opportunities to be tested because after going through the test you become stronger. So the more tests – the stronger you become.

Stand firm and determined not to quit during the test knowing that when you make it through you will be stronger and more committed to your goal.

Never let the outcome of a test discourage you from your goals. Always remember your desire is to achieve your goal and not any particular test.

Message #35

If You're Not Where You Want to Be, Maybe You're Not Dreaming Big Enough!

Dream Bigger!!!

That's right... let your imagination run wild and shoot for the stars.

Be a dreamer and DREAM BIGGER. When you walk down the street look towards the heavens and DREAM.

No one has ever achieved GREATNESS by accident. Sometimes we can be at the right place at the right time and something good can happen to us, but true accomplishment is expected, deliberate and planned.

It may not happen when you want... but it's RIGHT ON TIME when it happens.

Be careful not to compare yourself with someone great right now if you're not where you want to be. But go back in time and compare yourself with that person when they were getting started. You'll be surprised at where some great people were when they got started.

Remember, Setbacks are a chance to reaffirm your goals and Commitment is the foundation of all Success.

See Message #10 - "Burn the Ships"

Message #36

Expect To Win... It's Not Luck

Luck is randomly drawing your name out of a barrel of 1,000 names. You win because you expect to win.

You win because you are prepared.

You win because you actually "Know-You-Know" what you're doing.

You win because you hate Losing.

You win because you're sick and tired of losing and not getting what you want.

You win because you finally believe in yourself.

You win because you finally believe it's OK to be on top and stand above the competition.

You win because you've worked too hard and sacrificed too much to let it go.

You win because you actually plan and expect to WIN.

Somebody's got to win… Why not YOU!

Does this sound like luck?

Message #37

Two-Thirds of All Placebos Work!

What Does This Suggest About the Power of Expectation... Suggestion... Positive Thinking?

What is a Placebo?

A Placebo is a fake treatment for some medical problem that sometimes improves a patient's condition simply because the person has the expectation and belief that it will work.

Researchers have been studying the placebo effect for decades. In 1955, researcher H.K. Beecher published his groundbreaking paper "The Powerful Placebo," in which he concluded that across the 26 studies he analyzed, an average of 32 percent of patients responded to the placebo treatment.

Wow!

A more updated study published April 2012 by the Harvard Medical School concluded that up to two-thirds of placebos given to respondents had the desired effect.

What's your Placebo? Find one... create one... talk yourself into one. All you need is a reason, any reason, however flimsy or illogical, and your mind does the rest. Tell yourself "You're The Greatest" like Muhammad Ali.

Expectation is not Hoping for something. Just say it once and listen to how it sounds. "I EXPECT to succeed"... "I HOPE to succeed."

Which sounds more convincing and believable... something you can wrap your brain around.

Hope sounds like LUCK to me. Luck is getting your name pulled out of a group of 1,000 names. Don't say "Good Luck" to anyone anymore. We don't need more luck. We need more preparation, training and skills that will give us the belief and expectation that we will succeed.

Put the ball in the court of the person and say instead of "Good Luck Joe or Jane"... say "may the best Man or Woman win." Winning and Success has nothing to do with Luck. Yes, there may be a lucky break or undeserved call that goes your way, but ultimately to win and succeed one must confidently and deliberately pursue and seize the prize.

Muhammad Ali never said "I Think I'm the Greatest". He completely duped himself into believing He Was The Greatest and that he couldn't be beat. (See Message #12)

Message #38

Are You Ready to Break?

"Adversity, Pain and Bad Things Cause Some Men to Break and Others to Break Records!"
-- William Arthur Ward

We all have adversity, pain and bad things happen in our lives. That's right, everybody. The rain falls on the rich, the poor, the weak, the strong, the happy, the sad, the young, the old all the same… there's no difference.

Adversity, Pain and Bad Things are equal opportunity employers. They work everybody! The real question is not "will Adversity, Pain and Bad Things happen to you?" but rather "how you will deal with it when it happens to you?" Because it will happen to you!!!

Some of us have more adversity, pain and bad things than others but to pay attention to that is like complaining to the police officer that other people were speeding too when he pulls you over. You were still speeding regardless of how many people were speeding. See, by nature we all want to be in the same boat, even if it's sinking. Instead of climbing out of the boat and letting go of our pain and refocusing, we settle in and find others that want to talk about their pain too.

Misery Loves Company. DEAL WITH YOUR SITUATION with NO EXCUSES or JUSTIFICATIONS!

What separates us is how we deal with Adversity, Pain and Bad Things.

ARE YOU GOING TO LET PAIN, ADVERSITY AND BAD THINGS BREAK YOU or ARE YOU GOING TO USE THESE THINGS TO MAKE YOU BETTER THAN YOU WERE BEFORE?

GO BREAK SOME RECORDS NOW!

"If thou faint in the day of adversity, thy strength is small" – Proverbs 24:10

Message #39

Do You Always Get What You Want?

Of Course Not! Nobody Gets What They Want All of the Time.

Do You Always Get What You Get? Always! And Absolutely! I learned this very important life principle from a very special person in my life.

True power ultimately lies in what we get.

If we deal with what we get then we are dealing in the Truth and Reality.

When most people don't get what they want they waste even more time coming up with excuses, complaining and justifications. This is unproductive.

When you can honestly deal with what you get then you can effectively plan a different strategy to get what you really want.

This is not just a play on words but a play on your attitude.

Remember…You Don't Always Get What You Want… But You Always Get What You Get.

Message #40

Being Ordinary is Not an Option

If you want more of whatever it is you want more of… put the EXTRA in front of your Ordinary Effort and make it an EXTRAORDINARY Effort!

It's usually that little "EXTRA" effort that makes all the difference in getting what you want versus not getting what you want.

Consider this:

- It's not the size or cost of a house that make it a home, but instead it's the loving touches inside that cost nothing.

- A bag lunch made up of left overs can be a gourmet meal with a love note tucked inside.

- Candles turns a regular meal into an occasion.

- Studying just 1 more hour a day all semester can put you on the dean's list.

- Training just 1 more hour a day can make you a champion.

Doing anything just a little more each day can make a HUGE difference in the final outcome.

Doing more than required or expected will make your life EXTRAORDINARY!!!

Message #41

All Give Some… But Some Give All

In life, by default, we all have to give at least a certain amount of effort and passion to whatever it is we do.

The Key to true Happiness, Contentment and Fulfillment is to not merely Live By Default but by Being 100% Committed and Giving 100% effort to your endeavors.

Consider This:

Do you find that the more you give to someone in need the happier and more fulfilled you are? It's this relationship of giving 100% that creates more than 100% in power, effort, success, and ultimately fulfillment in life.

As a child I knew my parents would give me their last dime (and anything else in support of me) and no matter what I did they would always help and support me 100% (even though they may not have always agreed with me.) Most importantly they were 100% committed to my success with no judgment attached to the outcome (people that truly love you can do this.) 100% commitment and support of someone with no judgment attached to the outcome, creates high degrees of personal confidence which ultimately leads to the highest achievements.

Being 100% committed and supportive of someone else's effort (with no judgment) may be the catalyst that inspires them to a level of commitment that takes them to another level. It may even make them a 3-Time World Champion!

Our great men and women that serve and protect our country in the armed forces go into it knowing that they one day they may give their lives in the line of duty (a 100% commitment demanding a 100% effort.) Doesn't giving 100% create your greatest commitment?

When you're committed at the highest level, your effort, performance, and results will be at the highest level.

Don't Live Life by Default.

Message #42

It Only Matters What *YOU* Believe

In the 2017 NCAA Division 1 Wrestling Tournament held in St Louis, Missouri, only 50% of the #1 seeds actually won! Not only did the other 50% out perform their seeds – they were huge underdogs.

Consider These Facts:

At 125 & 133 pounds, the winners Darrian Cruz from Lehigh and Cory Clark from Iowa were both seeded 4th.

At 165, the winner Vincenzo Joseph, a redshirt freshman, from Penn State was seeded 3rd and had lost previously to his finals opponent only a few weeks earlier.

At 174, Mark Hall, a true freshman, from Penn State, seeded 5th came through the championships victorious wrestling what appeared to be up a weight class (from 165) when he was pulled out of redshirt status to fill the 174 pound slot.

At 184, the seemingly unstoppable #1 seed, senior and 2x NCAA Champion, Gabe Dean, from Cornell was upset by #2 seed Penn State sophomore, Bo Nickal.

You can choose your future.

Message #43

Just How Good Do You Have To Be?

It's not good enough that you learn your craft so well that you get it right most of the time... You need to learn your craft so well that you can't get it wrong!

I learned that there's a big difference between the two from John Taylor, a high school teammate from my alma matter, Chardon High School.

What do I mean by this?

Learning something well enough that we get it right most of the time still leaves room for mistakes and errors. After all, nobody's perfect, right?

Wrong... You CAN be perfect!

You may say "well isn't that good enough?" Well most people might say that it is good enough. This level of proficiency requires a great deal of effort to maintain because there are let downs in performance every now and then, and it is difficult to manage the highs and lows.

When you push beyond mere consistency to the level of perfection is when you become unbeatable.

At this level you don't know how to fail (or lose.)

You're not concerned about whether you will win or lose, succeed or fail... but your focus and attention turns towards how dominant your wins or successes will be.

Think of how your attitude would be if you didn't

have to worry about whether or not you were going to win or succeed; but rather all your focus could be concentrated on "how easily am I going to win or succeed."

Message #44

The Power Of NOW!

This very moment is the only thing you can really control. It's called "RIGHT NOW!" That's it! You only have control of THIS MOMENT IN TIME.

Consider these truths:

YOU can't change the PAST and YOU can't predict FUTURE events.

You CAN, however, have a great impact on future events by what you do RIGHT NOW!

OUR LIFE AS IT STANDS RIGHT NOW IS A SUM TOTAL OF ALL THE CHOICES, EFFORTS, AND ACTIONS WE'VE MADE AT EVERY MOMENT IN TIME OF OUR LIFE!!!

Think about everything that's happened to you in your life thus far: the GOOD, the BAD, and the UGLY. Weren't these outcomes directly related to the choices, efforts (or lack there of) and actions YOU'VE made.

Even if you got struck by lightning, isn't it because you chose to be in that place at that time? Everything that happens to us is caused ultimately be what we choose, our actions, and our efforts.

So think about the GREAT power we have in the NOW. How many times have we done or said something and immediately said, "I wish I wouldn't have done that" or "I wish I wouldn't have said that."

How many times have we said "I wish I would have studied more so I would have been better prepared for the test I just flunked"; or "I wish I would have _____ more so I would have _____". You fill in the blanks involving something you wished you would have done. You get the idea.

SO PUT YOUR GREATEST THOUGHT, EFFORT AND CONSIDERATION IN WHAT YOU ARE ABOUT TO "THINK-DO-OR SAY" RIGHT NOW!!!

Live in the NOW, because THAT'S THE ONLY THING YOU CAN CONTROL.

Message #45

Sometimes You Have to Go To The Deep Water to Catch the Big Fish!

By Staying in the Shallow Water (where it's safe) You'll Only Catch the Small Fish.

Get in the boat and leave the safety and comfort of the shore and go after the really BIG fish.

The further you go out the deeper the water and the more risk and uncertainty you'll find.

The further you go out the more doubt and fear of the unknown.

Staying on the shore you'll be sure to catch some fish... really small ones though.

Are really small ones OK with you? Or do you want the really BIG ones?

There is no EASY way to learn to do this. The way I learned to swim is the YMCA instructor made me walk out on the end of the diving board and told me to jump in. When I wouldn't jump in he came towards me (I thought to comfort me because I was nervous and almost in tears from being scared.) Guess what he did... THE S.O.B. THREW ME IN!

I thought I had only one option and that was to get to the side the best way I could. I didn't quite make it and Mr. Clark jumped in and got me out.

Guess what Mr. Clark did next? THE S.O.B. MADE ME DO IT AGAIN.

This time I was smart enough to jump myself so I could aim for the side and have only a few strokes to get to the side.

When your options are removed you FIND A WAY…YOU LEARN QUICK… YOU TRY HARDER… YOU PRAY HARDER (you make all kinds of deals and promises to GOD)… YOU PLAIN AND SIMPLE GET IT DONE!

The point is… you must challenge yourself by putting yourself in pressure situations… over and over and over again. Only then will you be putting yourself to the test. Test yourself… see what happens… you might surprise yourself.

IF YOU WANT TO RUN WITH THE BIG DOGS… YOU HAVE TO LEARN TO PEE IN THE TALL GRASS!!! (I Don't really know what that means but I heard it once and I kind of liked it.)

Message #46

Logic You're Not Wanted Here!

If Only We Could Have the Faith of a Little Child and Believe in Our Dreams...

Consider These Thoughts from Some Accomplished People.

I tell people I'm too stupid to know what's impossible. I have ridiculously large dreams, and half the time they come true. – Debi Thomas, World Figure Skating Champion.

Ideals (like Dreams) are like the stars: we never reach them, but like the mariners of the sea, we chart our course by them. – Carl Schurz, Missouri Senator from 1869 to 1875.

If one advances confidently in the directions of his dreams, and endeavors to live the life which he has imagined, he will meet with a success unexpected in common hours. – Henry David Thoreau, an American essayist, poet, and practical philosopher.

I have had dreams, and I have had nightmares. I overcame the nightmares because of my dreams. – Jonas Salk, American Biologist and Physician best known for the research and development of the first effective polio vaccine.

Every day is another chance to make your dreams come true. – Anonymous

Great love and great achievements involve great risk. – Anonymous

Do not follow where the path leads. Rather, go where there is no path and leave a trail. – Ralph Waldo Emerson

Dreams defy all reason and logic so you don't have to justify them…just believe in them. – Lee Kemp, 3-Time World Champion & Youngest American World Wrestling Champion.

**Message #47
A. A. I.**

If you were pretending to be what ever it is you're aspiring to be, HOW WOULD YOU ACT?

That's my question for YOU.

In my case, as a young wrestler back in the 70's I had the good fortune and opportunity to be in the presence of Dan Gable – arguably the person that's had the single greatest impact on wrestling in this country.

Gable's impact reached deep to all of us young wrestling wannabes. I was 15 years old when I went to a wrestling camp Gable was teaching. It was the summer of 1972. That summer Gable won the Olympic Gold medal in Munich Germany.

Gable had such an impact on me that I started to ACT AS IF…. I WAS DAN GABLE. That's right. I started to pretend I was Dan Gable.

With that idea came a huge amount of responsibility. I started to do what I saw Gable do at that camp (he was in his final training for the Olympics so he was very focused and intense.)

WOW! THAT PUT ME INTO A DIFFERENT WORLD! … I MEAN I WAS ON A DIFFERENT PLANET FROM EVERYONE ELSE!

There were times I wanted to NOT BE DAN GABLE. I was putting myself through some killer workouts and felt tremendous pressure. At times I didn't think it was worth it.

BUT SOMETHING INTERESTING HAPPENED.
I started to win more. You get the picture. It wasn't hard to convince myself that I was on the right tract. I went on to do a lot of winning in wrestling because of Dan Gable.

REMEMBER ALL I DID WAS SPEND SOME TIME IN HIS PRESENCE. I didn't know him and he didn't even remember that specific camp where I met him.

So I ask you this question. If you were pretending to be what ever it is you're aspiring to be, HOW WOULD YOU ACT? WHAT ADDITIONAL THINGS WOULD YOU DO?

If someone were watching you would they be able to characterize you as someone who was at the Top of their profession?

ACT AS IF ...(If you haven't figured it out yet that's what the A. A. I. stands for...)

Message #48

Positive Thinking Isn't Enough!

POSITIVE BELIEVING is what we NEED to get the job done....

There's a Huge Difference Between Positive Thinking and Positive BELIEVING!

Was Muhammad Ali a positive thinker or a positive BELIEVER? Like him or not the guy was mentally "ROCK SOLID". Muhammad Ali didn't go around saying I think I'm the greatest, I think I'm the greatest. He used to say – I'm the greatest period.

Let's just talk about the difference between positive thinking and positive believing for a minute. To illustrate the point I'll start with this story I heard from Dr. Rob Gilbert, co-author with me of the "Psychology of Winning Wrestling" audio CD series.

Dr. Gilbert tells the story of a Frenchman named Philippe who was an unusual type of athlete. He was a high wire walker. Way back in the fall of 1928 Philippe was attempting to become the first high wire walker ever to walk the high wire across Niagara Falls.

So the big day came and there were thousands of people on each side of the Falls to watch. Philippe was on the ramp on one side and the high wire was set up. Now Philippe wasn't like the high wire walkers you see in the circus that use a long pole for balance. Philippe used a wheelbarrow with 200 pounds of bricks in it.

So Philippe gets on the ramp on one side and he

slowly but masterfully starts crossing the Falls with his wheelbarrow. He got about halfway and then he suddenly stopped and started shaking back and forth. Then miraculously he regained his balance and went all the way to the other side.

He gets to the other side, gets this huge standing ovation and then after the ovation dies down the people start leaving. The journalists get to him and they start asking him question after question.

After they were all questioned out Philippe pointed to a young journalist and said, "Let me ask you a question." The journalist said sure. He said do you think I can take my wheelbarrow and go back to the other side? And the journalist said – of course I think you can, you're master of the high wire, of course I think you can. Philippe said – Let me ask you one more thing. Do you actually believe I can take my wheelbarrow and go back to the other side? The journalist said – totally, I have total confidence, I totally, 100% believe you can do it, you're a master of the high wire, I totally believe you can do it.

Philippe said fine. He dumped all the bricks out of his wheelbarrow and pointed to the journalist and said – If you really believe it get in the wheelbarrow.

This right here is where the rubber hits the road folks…So if you really, really, really believe in yourself, you'll take action. If you really, really, really believe you can become a champion you'll really go for it… **Now that's what I'm talking about!**

Message #49

The Single Biggest Mistake That Keeps Most People From Getting Motivated

Where Does Motivation Come From… and How Do We Get Motivated?

We get motivated by the desire to do SOMETHING… ANYTHING!

The desire to do something can also be the desire to achieve SOMETHING. This can also be called a GOAL!

The smaller the goal the smaller the motivation… AND YOU'RE NO DIFFERENT THAN ANYBODY ELSE.

THE BIGGER THE GOAL THE BIGGER THE MOTIVATION… AND YOU'RE STANDING ALONE WITH YOUR VISION. Think about this for a moment.

Also, when you're motivated, you automatically become excited.

BIGGER THE MOTIVATION… THE BIGGER THE EXCITEMENT. THE BIGGER THE EXCITEMENT… THE BIGGER THE PASSION, ACHIEVEMENT and REWARD!

That's it…. THE ONE BIGGEST MISTAKE THAT PEOPLE MAKE IS THEY SET THEIR GOALS TOO SMALL.

Message #50

A Technique You Can Use Right Now to Relieve Stress and Relax

Release the Natural Tranquilizers in Your Body...

Most things in life you force yourself to do. You go to school, work, practice, take a shower... whatever. It's a never ending process of force, force, force, force, force.

But try to force yourself to fall asleep; you can't... you just fall asleep.
Try to force yourself to breathe... If you had to make yourself breathe, inhale, exhale, then you wouldn't have a chance to do anything else. So the whole thing is it's a "letting" process, you just let it happen. You don't force it to happen.

In order to make yourself relax, YOU COULD JUST LET IT HAPPEN. How do we do it? It's easier than you think.

It starts with our breathing. Notice there are three parts to our breathing; inhalation, exhalation and then there's a slight pause.

And just notice that this is happening naturally, you're not making it happen, it's just happening involuntarily.

This is the technique: In your mind link up your breathing with a wave. So as you inhale you see and hear a big, beautiful wave coming in and crash. As you exhale, you see and hear the wave go out to sea.

Then there's a slight pause with the breathing and a

slight pause with the wave. And so the wave is linked with your breathing and the breathing is linked with the wave.

And just as with the wave when it comes into shore, it's bringing fresh, clean, clear water to the shore. As you're inhaling, you're bringing fresh, clean, clear, relaxing energy into your body.

Upon the exhalation the wave is going out to sea. The wave is taking any debris from shore out to sea. When you are exhaling, you have the opportunity to let any negative thoughts, stressing feelings or emotions to leave your body. Then there's a slight pause with the breathing and a slight pause with the wave.

A very simple exercise and you could do this just for a few minutes. Just to take the edge off any anxiety or stress you have. Just get in touch with your breathing.

You should practice this and just like anything else, the more you do it, the better you become at it. It's important to realize you have these natural tranquilizers inside your body, these powerful tranquilizers that could allow yourself to relax.

Message #51

INTIMIDATION

The word Intimidation has meaning for everyone. If you know how to intimidate people you can make it work for you. If you get intimidated, it will destroy you.

So what is intimidation? What is it that just makes you feel timid and scared? What makes that little voice in your mind say "this is too much for me, I can't face this."

I mean it just saps you of your strength. So you want to see an example of INTIMIDATION… just watch the stare down before any of Mike Tyson's fights (his early fights… especially his fight with Michael Spinks and Larry Holmes.)

Mike Tyson was a superior heavyweight champion but Nobody ever mentioned that for a heavyweight champion Mike Tyson was rather small in stature. I mean he's a very, very small man for a heavyweight fighter. Everybody he fights is a head taller than him but he does the intimidating.

Being intimidating is not about size it's about what's in your mind. Look at how intimidating Notre Dame football was during their reign and more recently Ohio State football. In wrestling I was there to witness the intimidation of the Iowa Hawkeyes during the Gable era… and now most recently the Sanderson era with Penn State. They intimidate their opponents just because of the aura around them. Some people think it's the uniform, some people think it's the tradition. Whatever it is, intimidation works.

Now, what you have to do to overcome intimidation is to practice not being intimidated. So let me ask you this. Did you ever have a teacher in school that you were afraid to talk to… a boss, a boy, a girl, dad, mom whatever?

Do you know what my assignment for you is? Go talk to that teacher. Go talk to that boss, Go talk to that person. I want you to do things that intimidate you and see what happens?

The more you do things that intimidate you, the less you'll be intimidated. So you ask the boss for the raise, ask the girl out for a date… the boss says no… the girl say no. The whole goal wasn't to just get the raise or get a yes from the girl… the whole goal was to do that confrontation, just to get the nerve to do it. The whole goal is to just confront the fear, confront the intimidation.

So that's what we're talking about. Practice putting yourself in situations where you're intimidated and then deal with it. And just like any fear, the more you confront the fear, the fear will lessen.

Message #52

How do you get a Breakthrough?

The First Real Success... How do we get it when we've failed so many times before?

We all have to realize that we don't always get what we want... but we always get what we GET.

The key here is to go to your last breath BELIEVING that you can and will SUCCEED! It is this mind set that keeps you in a position to BREAKTHROUGH when the moment or opportunity comes.

Just ask anyone that has had great success if it happened overnight. They'll tell you that it was with great struggle and hardship that they got their breakthrough. The key here is to continually find new ways to keep positive and motivated in the face of failure or falling short.

IT ISN'T EASY. But your breakthrough will come... it may not come when you want... BUT IT'S RIGHT ON TIME!

Message #53

How do you make a CHANGE in your LIFE?

It's All About Being Able to Change...

When you change your thinking, You change your beliefs;

When you change your beliefs, You change your expectations;

When you change your expectations, You change your attitude;

When you change your attitude, You change your behavior;

When you change your behavior, You change your performance;

When you change your performance, You change your life!

>- Dr. Walter Doyle Staples,
>(http://www.doctorstaples.com/)

Message #54

Take Care of Yourself...

Make Sure You Are Getting the Best Nutrition and Getting Enough Rest!

That means eating right – good "whole foods"-- and going to bed and getting at least 7-10 hours of uninterrupted "deep" sleep every night.

Why is this important? Your body runs on the nutrition you give it… much like your car. Bad gas in = bad performance out. Your body runs much the same way.

If you eat poorly and get inadequate nutrition, your body suffers. You may not feel it now… but as you get older you will… guaranteed.

Athletes need to be especially concerned about this because they are relying on their bodies to perform at state, national & world class levels, and too often athletes take nutrition lightly.

Without proper sleep and nutrition, the body can't perform optimally.

Message #55

Focus on the win, not the opponent.

Visualize the VICTORY not the PRESSURE you feel…

You have to completely embrace the idea that with all accomplishments there is PRESSURE. In fact, the greater the accomplishment, the greater the pressure.

Tennis superstar Serena Williams said recently: "It's a privilege to be in that situation where you actually have pressure on your shoulders, as opposed to not having that pressure."

I'll take it a step further. "PRESSURE IS THE PRIVILEGE OF CHAMPIONS!"

If you really want to be a champion start accepting that feeling pressure is a privilege… a sort of "rite of passage."

Typically, when most people feel pressure it's because they're thinking about an opponent. The more you think about your opponent the more you'll feel the pressure.

But the opponent doesn't matter really. If you really want the victory you're going to have to beat everybody anyway.

When I competed I didn't think about my opponents too much. The pressure I felt was from wanting to be the best at what I did… WANTING TO BE THE CHAMPION.

Message #56

Living Backwards in Time...

Live into Your Dreams!

The first time I heard the phrase "Living Backward in Time" I questioned what it meant. I thought it had something to do with living in the past... something we definitely don't want to do.

However, once I fully understood what it meant I immediately embraced the concept. Here are my steps for Living Backwards in time:

1. Start with the Goal you want to attain. Visualize and embrace the goal as if you have already attained it. Know that it's yours.

2. Once you've visualized and embraced the goal ask yourself "how did I get here?"

3. Write down all the things you did to get to your Goal... the training, preparation, studying, discipline, sacrificing, etc....

4. From that point "Live Backward in Time" to the present (this is the point you're at right now) doing all the things necessary to make sure the future events unfold the way you envisioned them.

5. Each day "TiVo" your life and watch the replay of your past days actions, accessing whether your actions really do align with the things you've outlined in #3 above as the "way you got to your goal."

6. TAKE ACTION!

7. If your actions of the past day aren't in line with Step #3 above make a CHANGE!

CHANGE THE NEXT EPISODE of your upcoming day's actions so that you are always on track!

DREAM BIG!

Message #57

The Two Brothers…

The Power of DREAMING BIG!

This is a story about two brothers as told by Dr. Rob Gilbert, co-author with me of the audio CD Series entitled, "The Psychology of Winning Wrestling."

Two brothers went to a motivational lecture on goal setting and after the lecture one of the brothers said, "You know, why don't we set income goals for the next year? I'll write down my goal on an index card and seal it in an envelope and you write down your goal and you won't tell me, on an index card and put it in an envelope. A year from now we'll see what happens."

So one brother writes down $50,000 and seals it in his envelope. His brother doesn't know what he wrote down. The other brother wrote down $1,000,000.

A year later they got together and the brother that wrote down $50,000 was all excited and opens his envelope and says, "This stuff works! I made $52,000 – this is the most money I ever made."

Then nonchalantly the other brother opens his envelope and he said, "Well, unfortunately I only made it halfway to my goal."

So the brother that wrote down $50,000, even though he achieved more than 100% of his goal, made ten times less than the brother who set his goal for $1,000,000.

Dr. Rob Gilbert says we should definitely DREAM BIG! That's what I'm talking About!!!

Message #58

Thinking vs. Doing…

This is the one thing most of us do too much of...

Most of our time and energy is spent thinking about doing something rather than actually doing it.

Thinking about doing something yields entirely different results than actually doing something.

Thinking is way overrated. Most of us overthink things, and as a result never get moving to actually doing the things we were thinking about.

99% of why we don't accomplish things in life is because we never get to them.

The more we think, the more we talk ourselves out of the thing we want.

In fact, the circumstances we find ourselves in reflect back to what we were thinking.

Keep your thinking short, direct and to the point!

Message #59

Keep a Consistent and Focused Goal Oriented Attitude!

Attitude is defined as "a mental position (or a feeling or emotion) with regard to something".

Most of us are quick to let a negative circumstance change our attitude and feelings about something.

For example, something happens we don't like…we get a strong, negative attitude about it that changes our thinking.

This type of attitude reacts to the circumstance. Unfortunately, when your attitude is determined by the circumstance, consistent high level performance is impossible.

REMEMBER, WE ARE ALWAYS IN THE CIRCUMSTANCE THAT WE ARE IN!

So don't fret over your circumstance. Circumstances will always happen.

Bad Stuff Happens all the time but it doesn't have to negatively impact our ATTITUDE.

Instead focus your ATTITUDE on a GOAL… A goal that does not change… A goal that you are Passionate about!

Message #60

Are You Putting It All On The Line…?

There's no Limit to What You Can Do, But to Find Out What You Can Do You Must First Put It All On The Line…

The reason most people don't put it all on the line is because the very act of putting it on the line exposes any weaknesses and, of course, any strengths.

Putting it on the line means going all out… holding nothing back.

HOW ELSE WILL YOU KNOW WHAT YOU REALLY CAN DO? HOW ELSE WILL YOU BE ABLE TO MAKE ANY CHANGES BASED ON EXPOSED WEAKNESSES?

You need to know what your strengths are just as you must know what your weakness are.

To win at the highest levels you must know what your strengths and weakness are and you must practice this every day.

Put it … All On The Line (AOTL)… every day. You can look at this another way… Put you're <u>A</u>SS <u>O</u>n <u>T</u>he <u>L</u>ine … every day!

Message #61

Live Life Today as if Today was all you Had...

Because all we really have is NOW, That's all we really can Control. Tomorrow is not promised.

I had the good fortune to meet a great man recently. He was a wise man full of years with a lot of life experience, but unfortunately he was dying. In fact, when I met him he would only be alive for 14 more days. But I noticed this man had no regrets. He was at peace with his life.

After spending some time with this man I learned very quickly that he really loved life and lived life to the fullest! I also came to this powerful revelation…

All we have control of is this very moment in time; and we have to get the most out of this moment. This moment in time is NOW!

When time runs out… that's it… there's nothing more we can do in this earthly realm.

All that we accomplish in life, no matter how long we live, no matter how much success we have, no matter how much we love and are loved, no matter what plans we have and had, no matter how full our life is or was… At the end we all will ponder, did we accomplish what we set out to do in our lives? Did we take full advantage of all the "NOWS" we had.

No matter what, it all comes to an END!

TIME TAKES CARE OF EVERYTHING AND EVERYBODY!

All of us will one day run out of time.

So I got to thinking… what is it that I still want to do with my life?

As I thought about this it became apparent to me that we really don't have any control of our plans… we only have control of NOW.

Remember the saying "the best laid plans of mice and men…." you know the rest.

Take advantage of this very moment. Make something really special of this moment. That's what I was able to do in my wrestling career… I took advantage of every moment and lived each moment in wrestling (as it related to competition, training & learning) as if it were my last and as a result I was successful at it.

This philosophy will work at anything we want to accomplish in life.

Message #62

Winning Takes on Many Forms – Bob Wieland is a Winner!

Wake up every day with a Purpose, Goal or Objective for the Day. Then Go After It!

How many people have biked or walked across America? Bob Wieland has done both ... with no legs.

More than 30 years ago Bob Wieland lost his legs and nearly his life in Vietnam. Faced with seemingly insurmountable adversity, he persevered and made a miraculous recovery.

He has since been on a mission to show people that "through faith in God, determination, and dedication, a person can achieve anything." He has always also said, "The joy is in the journey."

A list of Bob's achievements include:

- A three-year, eight-month and six-day walk across America on his hands.

- He completed the grueling Iron Man Triathlon (2.4-mile swim, 112-mile bike ride, and 26-mile marathon) using only his arms.

- At age 57, he finished the Los Angeles marathon using only his hands and torso.

Bob literally has no peers in human achievement.

People Magazine called Bob Wieland "one of the six most amazing Americans of the past 20 years."

THIS IS TRULY AMAZING!!!

I DON'T WANT TO HEAR EVER AGAIN SOMEONE TELL ME HOW HARD OR HOW DIFFICULT SOMETHING IS.

MY MINDSET IS CHANGED FOREVER!!!

WHAT'S YOUR PURPOSE FOR THE DAY?

Message #63

Deal With It!!!

Excuses...Excuses...Excuses!

I hear a lot of conversations about why things don't get done. Please... STOP the conversations. Stop the EXCUSES. Stop the EXPLANATIONS. Stop the JUSTIFICATIONS!

All that stuff is really the outgrowth of our FEAR.

Fear causes us to make excuses (i.e. explaining and justifying why something did or did not happen.)

NO EXPLANATIONS OR JUSTIFICATIONS! PLEASE... JUST ACTION. You've heard of "Show me the money" ... well... SHOW ME THE ACTION with no conversations!

In life for every decision we make we are either GETTING something for it... or AVOIDING something for it. The latter is living by default. The former is ACTION-oriented living with purpose.

DEAL WITH YOUR FEARS AND TAKE ACTION TOWARDS YOUR FUTURE.

Message #64

Remember to ALWAYS STAY CALM

Staying calm provides the framework for all success.

Over the years I've noticed 4 distinct principles that all very successful people seemed to have. I've noticed this in my own success too, and realized that these 4 principles are essential for really Great Success. All 4 must be present and active for the formula to work. Here they are:

1. Commitment – Before any achievement can occur there must first be Commitment.

- What is Commitment Really? I define it as showing up every day.
- Showing up every day… Is that enough?
- Lots of reasons to be committed to something i.e., it's my job and I have to, or else I'll get fired.
- Commitment does not translate into success and achievement.
- It has been said that – "Half of life is showing up every day" But Showing up is not enough.

2. Acceptance – The next principle along the path to really GREAT achievement is Acceptance.

- Acceptance is a person's assent (or approval) to the REALITY of a situation and as it relates to success, performance and achievement it is the Recognition of the process and/or conditions necessary. Often time this can be a Negative, Hard or Uncomfortable series of necessary obstacles and/or processes in between you and the really Great success and performance you want. What this really is is the acceptance of all the "WORK" required for the success, and I mean ALL THE WORK. Not just the work you like or the work you can tolerate. It's all the WORK. This is uncomfortable and this is WHERE MOST PEOPLE QUIT and go back to just being committed.

- Get comfortable being uncomfortable and learn to accept doing ALL THE WORK!

- Turn things you don't like into things you LOVE. (turn weakness into strengths)

- When I first started wrestling I didn't want to do the running, weight lifting and drilling to learn new moves. – I JUST WANTED TO WRESTLE IN PRACTICE. I knew I was talented and didn't think I needed to do those things to be successful. Oh, and let me add, I didn't want to "cut the weight" either. That was too hard. I knew I was good enough to wrestle up a weight and still have a chance to win the State Championship. So I wanted the short cut of not cutting the weight, because cutting the extra weight meant that I had to add extra workouts throughout the week on my own, in addition to the regular practices (which were very hard) to make the weight class.

- My coach pulled me aside one day and made me understand talent was not enough if I wanted to be a State Champion. I had to accept doing the running, weight lifting and drilling – and other things too like cutting the weight. I told my high school coach midway through the wrestling season my senior year that I wanted to move up a weight class – from 145 to 155 lbs. I had won the State title my junior year at 138 lbs. with an undefeated season and was undefeated thus far in my senior season, and somehow felt I needed (and deserved) a break from the "weight cutting". Well as I found out it really wasn't about "weight cutting" (let me say right here that I don't recommend or believe in excessive and drastic "weight cutting"). My coach knew I was good and I was still rapidly improving and acknowledged that I probably could win at the higher weight, but this is what he told me:

"I know you could probably win at the higher weight, but what got you here is all the hard work, and the extra workouts that I know you're doing at home at night after practice. I know you do extra running, weight lifting and calisthenics to get the weight off, and this has

gotten you into excellent condition and has made you mentally tough. Are you wanting to go up a weight so you don't have to do any of these extra things? Or is making the weight really too hard? He told me to go home that night and think about it and give my decision to him in the morning." Well, my high school coach nailed it and it hit me right between the eyes. I came in the next morning and told him I was staying at 145 lbs.

- A big part of acceptance is the Belief that the total commitment is good for you and absolutely essential and necessary.

Liking – moving quickly into **LOVING** – This is the Most critical principle along the path of achievement.

- Now there must be a feeling of pleasure and enjoyment for the TOTAL process involved in the attainment of the desired success or goal.

- Once the barrier of acceptance is broken then a funny and strange thing happens. You begin to like the tasks that you once hated or disliked. In my case I actually began to like the running, weight lifting and drilling.

- Another example in my own life was once I started doing all the work I started to like graduate school. Studying 5-6 hours a day to earn my MBA from the University of Wisconsin Graduate School of Business began to be something I looked forward to.

- "I've always had an intense **LOVE** for the process of doing what was necessary to win at the highest levels in wrestling".

Mastery – This is principle where all the FUN Begins.

- Defined as Possession or Display of great skill or knowledge that makes one a master of a subject or thing. Mastery is Demonstrated by actual DOING. This is not the time for talking about wanting to be great. Mastery is all about doing and Execution of the thing.

- I know of no "Masters" that didn't absolutely LOVE their craft and all that went into it.

Now, you probably are wondering what does all this have to do with staying calm.

Commitment **A**cceptance **L**oving **M**astery™

Message #65

Keep Believing in your Miracle.

***Don't quit the moment before your miracle…
your breakthrough… your SUCCESS!***

If you keep believing that your breakthrough will come then your success will come.

One way to keep your dream alive is to constantly visualize your success. Role-play it in your mind. Then step out of your mind and role-play your future success by acting it out. Really act it out!

As a young wrestler I used to make an award stand in my bedroom and role-play getting up on the #1 spot after hearing my name announced as the champion. Sounds corny but this stuff works.

Another way is to make a feature film of your success in your mind and create a "highlight" trailer and PLAY YOUR SUCCESS CONSTANTLY IN YOUR MIND!

Message #66

Want to be a true LEADER in anything?

For the true Leader, thinking outside the box is not enough… for the true leader THERE IS NO BOX.

What Exactly is a True Leader?

- The true leader Innovates; while others only administers what's already there.

- The true leader is an original while others attempt to copy.

- The true leader makes things happen while others ask "what happened"

- The true leader originates while others imitate.

- The true leader is intensely interested in continual personal and professional development while others simply maintain where they currently are.

- The true leader focuses on developing people because they know that's best way to get things done. Others focus on systems and structure.

- The true leader inspires trust while others rely on control.

- The true leader sees the "big picture" and has a long-range perspective while others maintain a short-range view and only see the immediate circumstance(s).

- The true leader asks "what" and "why" while others ask "how" and "when".

- The true leader challenges the status quo while others accept it.

- The true leader does the right thing while others do things right.

(This was adapted from "Becoming a Leader" – Warren Bennis.)

Message #67

Can You Take A Hit?

Measure a man by the opposition it takes to discourage him.

The above statement was written on a sign in our Wrestling Room at Wisconsin that I Looked at EVERYDAY.

As a college athlete I knew there would be obstacles to overcome everyday... i.e. injuries, tough practices, classes and grades, competition, you name it.

All I knew is that I wasn't going to quit and I was somehow going to be an NCAA Champion. I also knew that SUCCESS IS NEVER EASY.

I think Rocky Balboa said it well in *Creed*, the latest movie from that film franchise:

"Let me tell you something you already know. The world ain't all sunshine and rainbows. It's a very mean and nasty place, and I don't care how tough you are, it will beat you to your knees and keep you there permanently if you let it. You, me, or nobody is gonna hit as hard as life. But it ain't about how hard you hit. It's about how hard you can get hit and keep moving forward; how much you can take and keep moving forward. That's how winning is done! Now, if you know what you're worth, then go out and get what you're worth. But you gotta be willing to take the hits, and not pointing fingers saying you ain't where you wanna be because of him, or her, or anybody. Cowards do that and that ain't you. You're better than that! I'm always gonna love you, no

matter what. No matter what happens. You're my son and you're my blood. You're the best thing in my life. But until you start believing in yourself, you ain't gonna have a life".
- Rocky Balboa

Message #68

What You Do Today DOES Matter!

Have You Ever Ended Up Somewhere and Wonder How in the World Did I Get Here?

That is precisely the point. How Did I get here?!? This applies in Every Aspect of Life.
Like driving somewhere & getting lost and ending up somewhere you didn't want to be... Ending up with Friends, People, Spouse, Kids, Sickness, Disease, or a Job you don't really want to be with, etc., you name it...

Basically just not being happy with where you're at and/or the direction you're going!

I'm here to tell you that this just didn't happen by accident. It didn't just happen overnight or all of a sudden... IT HAPPENED OVER TIME FOLKS.

TIME is the Game Changer Here. It is either our friend or it is our enemy. It's ONE OR THE OTHER. Our choices, multiplied by TIME, happens to all of us. It happens to me and it happens to you.

The Key is recognizing when wrong choices are being repeated over TIME, heading us down a path we really don't' want... and STOP! Stop the train immediately! Reassess your GOALS and pick a different path. Sounds simple... but it's not.

Picking a different path means making a different CHOICE... Making a different DECISION... Making a CHANGE.

This is the GOLDEN NUGGET HERE: Your daily choices, decisions and actions when added up every day over TIME will always take us to our ACCOMPLISHMENTS and ACHIEVEMENTS. NO EXCEPTIONS.

I've analyzed literally thousands of successful people's daily actions (including mine) and concluded they were all on the straight and narrow path to their future accomplishments and success.

Any detour off the path by "wrong daily actions" compounded by time would have taken them grossly off course missing the success and accomplishments that was "gift wrapped" waiting for them (including me.)

So if you're asking yourself how did I get here, just play back the recorder of your life on a day-by day basis, up to this moment, and you will realize with crystal clarity exactly how you got here, and more importantly where your life is headed.

Want to change your life? Start today by changing what you do today and multiply your successful daily routine over TIME and I guarantee you will get the result your daily actions are pointing to.

NO MYSTERIES HERE - JUST CONSISTENCY.

REMEMBER, whatever happens to you, be sure, YOU are 100% responsible!

Message #69

**Don't Just Stand There…
MYA (MOVE YOUR ASS)!**

Dr. Rob Gilbert, Leading Sports Psychologist, coined the phrase GOYA (Get off your ASS.)

I'm coining the phase MYA (MOVE YOUR ASS.)

You must absolutely get up and start Moving! Not just anywhere... but Move in the direction of your GOALS.

YOU SHOULD KNOW WHAT YOU WANT... Right?! Once You Know that... START MOVING IN THAT DIRECTION.

Take a first step... then another... then another.

You've heard the saying... if you stumble and fall... Stumble and fall forward. NEVER BACKWARD. Fight hard not to go backward. For those of you that trade stocks, it's like setting a trailing STOP after you've made some gains. If your stops are tight and continually adjusted upward you can never lose what you've gained.

Set trailing stops in LIFE!

What are we really saying... By moving your ass you are creating an ACTION. When you create an action you are doing something.

Here's the golden nugget... YOU CAN ALWAYS (without exception) CONTROL YOUR ACTIONS... AND YOUR ACTIONS ARE INDEPENDENT OF YOUR FEELINGS, EMOTIONS OR THOUGHTS.

The trick is to make your actions move towards your goals (remember this is independent of how you feel.)

Example – doing something you don't like… but you know it is moving you in the direction you want (i.e., studying, lifting weights, working that 2nd job to pay for night school, or while in grammar school that job after school to pay for J Robinson's intensive camp, etc.)

It is by far easier to control and change what you DO (i.e., your actions) than it is to control and change your feelings, emotions or thoughts.

Successful people act even when they don't really want to. They take the feelings and emotions out of the equation.

They consistently live by GOYA and MYA.

Message #70

Are You Working to get Better... REALLY?

How serious are you at working to get better?

We all say we want to get better… but are we working at it REALLY?

Ask yourself these six things:

Are you taking advantage of every opportunity to get better?

Are you taking an honest assessment of where you're at right now? And more importantly are you DREAMING BIG and setting high goals?

Are you challenging yourself every day?

Are you "jumping in the ring" (in whatever arena you're in) with the best people every day and testing yourself?

Do you let down when you get tired or have a set back?

Do you let other people "break" you? Break your spirit, your will, your desires, your goals, your plans, your drive, your expectations…?

What I find is that most people really don't try that hard at being successful. They try a little bit and if they don't achieve immediate results, they may not quit, but they don't try as hard.

The incredible thing is that even when people experience some success from their efforts, I find that they still don't try that hard. I really don't understand this because I believe that is the key here.

Here's the nugget, don't miss it…

Get those little successes (from your effort) and stop and let yourself feel the high from it. You need to get addicted to it like a drug that you must have to live. This will drive you to want more. You will work hard at trying to get better… REALLY!

These little successes should be FRONT PAGE NEWS in your life.

I was at the Midlands wrestling tournament this past season and after the final match of one of the champions I saw him running behind the bleachers.

He continued running until he was called to the award stand. Then, after accepting his award he continued running.

I congratulated him on his championship and then I asked him why he was working out right now (of course I knew the answer.)

His answer is the essence of this post. Please pay attention to his answer….

He said I'M JUST TRYING TO GET BETTER!!!

This wrestler was a true sophomore, was 2nd in the NCAA's as a true freshman and recently won the Freestyle Senior Nationals beating a former world team member.

When he was interviewed after his match he again said I'M JUST TRYING TO GET BETTER!!!

This young man has the right idea about success!

Message #71

Ride the Wild Tiger!

Life is Like a Wild Tiger… You can either lie down and let it lay its paws on your head…. or YOU CAN SIT ON ITS BACK AND RIDE IT!

Heard this recently, don't know who the original author is, but it really impacted me in a big way and I wanted to share it.

I find in my own life the essence of this quote working. Who hasn't been knocked down by LIFE? … Nobody! We all Have… and guess what?… we will continue to be knocked down.

LIFE (or as the wise author of this quote has coined "The Wild Tiger") has dealt us all some hard times and will continue to rear its ugly head from time to time.

The really important questions is… are we going to let it (the circumstance that LIFE dealt) control us??? I love the way the way the author says "you can lie down and let it (LIFE's circumstance) lay its paw on your head."

In my own life, I stay beaten down until I decide to face the Tiger head on and RIDE IT… If I fall off I get back on… and back on… and back on… you get the picture.

Eventually I overcome it and RIDE THE TIGER. It's the same principle for achieving your Goals. Your Goal is the Wild Tiger.

Are you going to RIDE THE WILD TIGER???

Message #72

Don't Focus on Winning…

Although winning is the goal, you must focus on something else to truly achieve your success.

I recently read a short quote about Selling that really stuck with me. It went something like this:

"To sell more don't focus on what and how you can sell your customer… But instead focus on what you can do and how you can HELP your customer."

By doing that you will solve your customer's problems and flow right into selling them naturally. The best salespeople are Super Problem Solvers.

This quote got me thinking about my success in wrestling and lo and behold… I wasn't focused on winning as much as I was focused on GETTING BETTER!

That's it. I was focused on what I could do to get better and how could I get better each day rather than focusing on the end result of Winning.

It's simple… THE BETTER YOU GET… THE MORE YOU WIN!

FOCUS ON GETTING BETTER!

Message #73

Pretend You Have an "S" on Your Chest.

You're not really pretending… What you're doing is visualizing.

There is a Superman inside of all of us… But first we must discover him… and believe.

The difference between Clark Kent and Superman is their attitude and personality. Clark has one attitude and personality and Superman has another. It is the same with each of us. We all have to first realize we have a Superman inside us and then we must learn to develop and train our Superman.

When a job calls for Superman… Superman must show up. No excuses, it doesn't matter if there's no phone booth around.

This is called our Alter Ego. An alter ego (Latin, "the other I") is a second self, a second personality or persona within a person. When I trained and competed I was a totally different person than when I wasn't training or competing.

We all know Clark and Superman are the same person but we all know there is another side of Clark… and that is the Superman inside him.

Top athletes refer to this as bringing their "A" Game. But how do we guarantee ourselves we are bringing our "A" game… that Superman will show up?

"A" Games and "Superman Performances" are built on practice and training under pressure. What do I mean by this? Train and practice under pressure to perform at competition levels. Completely simulate the pressure of the competition and put pressure on yourself to perform at your highest levels.

Sometimes the difference between an "A" Game and a Superman performance is the extra hours invested in the preparation and training. Just an extra hour a day of training (when others have gone home) for a month adds up to 30 additional hours of training (or studying or whatever.)

Michael Jordan, the best basketball player that ever played the game, trained and practiced countless hours on the fundamentals of his game, because he knew he must train the "Superman" inside him.

When the day of your "Superman" event arrives could you use an extra 30 hours of preparation to make sure Superman arrives?

Message #74

The Key... Part 1.

"def. Focus (Photography): The action of adjusting the distance between the lens and subject to make light rays converge to form a clear and sharply defined image of the subject."

I get asked all the time by young wrestlers how I achieved success so quickly in wrestling.

To recap, I started wrestling in 9th grade and didn't make varsity until 10th grade. The next year in 11th grade I was the state champ beating both the defending state runner-up and state champ. State champ again the next year in 12th grade finishing the last two years undefeated. Won the Jr. Nationals (beating a future 3-time NCAA Div-I champion) and beat a Russian in a N.E. Ohio vs Russia Junior Dual. Next year as an 18 year old college freshman I lost an overtime split referees decision in NCAA Div-I finals. Next year, just 6 years after starting wrestling, beat Gable (he was the Olympic Champion 4 years earlier and was 26 years old) and and won NCAA Div-I championship, the 1st of three consecutive titles. Two years later was the youngest American Gold medalist in the world championships. Next year was America's first multiple-time world champion. Three years later was a 3-time world champion – the first American three-time world champion.

HOW?? is the most common question I get asked. Not just by wrestlers or athletes, but I find I get asked this HOW question by virtually everyone interested in HOW success is achieved.

For years I gave the canned answer of hard work, sacrifice, dedication, etc. But when I really thought about it I realized that it was all because of FOCUS.

I'll say it again... FOCUS!

Sounds simple but it's probably the hardest one thing to do on this earth... Especially with all the things pulling for our attention on a minute by minute basis 24/7.

The definition of Focus, as given at the beginning of this message, describes focus as related to photography, but I think it frames what Focus is in all things. It was especially true for me as an athlete.

How do you get "a clear and sharply defined image of the subject?" This is performed in photography by "adjusting the distance between the lens and subject." I relate this to focusing on a goal.

It's easier to believe you can accomplish something if you can actually "see it" clearly in your mind. If it's not clear in your mind, then it's harder to see and believe.

The clearly defined image of the subject is your GOAL. The LENS is your MIND's EYE. And adjusting the distance between these to form a clear and sharply defined image of the subject is the process of "fine tuning" your goal, or simply, how clearly you see your goal in your mind's eye.

It always amazed me that Eagles can clearly focus

on a mouse over a mile away... THAT'S FOCUS!

If the goal is fuzzy, then the effort and subsequent success is "fuzzy" too. For me my goals were laser sharp and crystal clear... I WAS SUPREMELY FOCUSED! Therefore, so was my effort that led to the success.

The clearer and more sharply defined your goal is in your mind's eye... the greater your FOCUS. The greater your focus, the greater your willingness to do all the things you KNOW you need to do to attain the goal (i.e. the hard work, sacrifice, dedication... etc.)

It becomes an unstoppable machine... FOCUS ... EFFORT... SUCCESS. Tune in your FOCUS and you'll have more SUCCESS.

Message #75

The Key… Part 2.

def. Habit: Adopting an acquired pattern of behavior and thought that becomes almost involuntary as a result of frequent repetition.

This definition beautifully describes what is absolutely essential to achieving success and it goes hand in hand with my previous message on FOCUS.

Focusing, as I previously mentioned, helps you to clearly visualize your goal. The big problem I see is people have a hard time maintaining their focus. I believe that life's distractions rob us of our focus. In fact, I believe that's the #1 cause of failure... DISTRACTIONS.

We all have a certain amount of focus, but what I've seen in myself and other people who've achieved success is an unwavering ability to "stay in the zone" and block out distractions. The greater your ability to block out any and all distractions, the greater is your potential for Success!

So then... how do we block any and all distractions? We must first develop a HABIT.

I believe before you can have FOCUS (and later success) you must have first created a consistent and distraction free environment through developing and "adopting an acquired pattern of behavior and thought that becomes almost involuntary as a result of frequent repetition." This behavior becomes a part of your focus.

When I was at my best as a wrestler, I simply could not be DISTRACTED. The HABIT that I adopted was to steer clear of negative people… negative thoughts… negative food… etc., and as a force of habit surrounded myself with only positive people… positive thoughts… positive food etc.

PEOPLE, THOUGHTS and FOOD I could control… and I did. I left out working hard for a reason. Most everybody that's serious about success Works Hard! It's not about Working Hard. It's all about STAYING FOCUSED!

How do you stay Focused?

Develop **H**ealthy **A**ttitudes that **B**ring **I**mpact **T**oday.

Conclusion
(Not) My Last Message

I believe achieving success ranks pretty high in the desires of most people. Unfortunately, few people every really venture too far out of their comfort zone, so consequently significant success rarely happens for most people.

In almost every motivational post in my book success requires a risk of failure. But success also requires a burning desire to succeed against the odds, and most importantly, the ability to continually stay motivated and focused that helps you reach your desired outcome.

My book is filled with success stories, inspirational messages and videos, antidotes and quotes from people from all walks of life, including my own personal thoughts that fueled my success. It is my hope that after reading this book you can find something to inspire you towards greatness!

To your Success!

For a collection of inspirational YouTube videos that I personally find empowering and additional Messages from me, please go to my website at **www.LeeKemp.com**.

www.ingramcontent.com/pod-product-compliance
Lightning Source LLC
Chambersburg PA
CBHW070639050426
42451CB00008B/217